Roger McGough

The Way Things Are

VIKING

For Isabel and Matthew,
Tom and Finn

VIKING

Published by the Penguin Group
Penguin Books Ltd, 27 Wrights Lane, London w8 5tz, England
Penguin Putnam Inc., 375 Hudson Street, New York, New York 10014, USA
Penguin Books Australia Ltd, Ringwood, Victoria, Australia
Penguin Books Canada Ltd, 10 Alcorn Avenue, Toronto, Ontario, Canada m4v 3b2
Penguin Books (NZ) Ltd, Private Bag 102902, NSMC, Auckland, New Zealand

Penguin Books Ltd, Registered Offices: Harmondsworth, Middlesex, England

First published 1999
1 3 5 7 9 10 8 6 4 2

Copyright © Roger McGough, 1999
The moral right of the author has been asserted

Set in 11.75/14.5pt Monotype Bembo
Typeset by Rowland Phototypesetting Ltd, Bury St Edmunds, Suffolk
Printed in Great Britain by Clays Ltd, St Ives plc

A CIP catalogue record for this book is available from the British Library

ISBN 0−670−88655−6

Contents

The Way Things Are

No, the candle is not crying, it cannot feel pain.
Even telescopes, like the rest of us, grow bored.
Bubblegum will not make the hair soft and shiny.
The duller the imagination, the faster the car,
I am your father and this is the way things are.

When the sky is looking the other way,
do not enter the forest. No, the wind
is not caused by the rushing of clouds.
An excuse is as good a reason as any.
A lighthouse, launched, will not go far,
I am your father and this is the way things are.

No, old people do not walk slowly
because they have plenty of time.
Gardening books when buried will not flower.
Though lightly worn, a crown may leave a scar,
I am your father and this is the way things are.

No, the red woolly hat has not been
put on the railing to keep it warm.
When one glove is missing, both are lost.
Today's craft fair is tomorrow's car boot sale.
The guitarist gently weeps, not the guitar,
I am your father and this is the way things are.

Pebbles work best without batteries.
The deckchair will fail as a unit of currency.
Even though your shadow is shortening
it does not mean you are growing smaller.
Moonbeams sadly, will not survive in a jar,
I am your father and this is the way things are.

For centuries the bullet remained quietly confident
that the gun would be invented.
A drowning surrealist will not appreciate
the concrete lifebelt.
No guarantee my last goodbye is au revoir,
I am your father and this is the way things are.

Do not become a prison-officer unless you know
what you're letting someone else in for.
The thrill of being a shower curtain will soon pall.
No trusting hand awaits the falling star,
I am your father, and I am sorry,
but this is the way things are.

What Happened to Henry

What happened to Henry Townsend that summer
still turns my stomach. Not long after the war
when barrage balloons had been cut loose
and coal was delivered by horse and cart

lads would chase the wagon up the street
and when the coalie wasn't looking
grab hold of the tailboard, and legs dangling
hang there for as long as they could.

According to one, Henry, head thrown back
and swinging too close to the edge,
had caught his foot between the spokes
of the rear left wheel. As it turned

his leg snapped in half. I heard the screams
three streets away. Not his, but his mother's,
who'd been gabbing on the corner.
Air-raid sirens to send us all scurrying.

The driver, ashen-faced beneath the coaldust
held fast the reins to prevent the horse
from moving, but nervous, it bucked
and strained and tried to pull away.

Glad to be of use, two men unbuckled the traces,
freed the horse and laid the shafts gently down.
A kitchen chair was brought out so that
Henry could take the weight off his leg.

★   ★   ★

Those are the facts and this is the picture:
Late one summer's afternoon in Seaforth
on a wooden chair on a cobbled street
a ten-year-old sits with his leg in a wheel.

His mother is crying, but not Henry.
He is stock-still. Against her blue pinny
his face has the pale luminescence of an angel.
A neighbour brings him out a drink of water,

cup and saucer, best china. No sign yet
of an ambulance. Not a policeman in sight.
Frantic, my gran arrives to chase me home.
(Compared to his sister, though, Henry got off light.)

What Happened to Dorothy

That's me on the left.
Page-boy in a velvet suit.
Four years old, blond curls and scowling.
Lucky horseshoe trailing.

That's Dorothy, Maid-of-Honour.
Though only three years older,
in her long white dress,
veil and floral tiara
she could be a teenager.

She never would be, though.

(It wasn't a road accident)
    Tin bath in the kitchen.
(It wasn't diphtheria)
    Pan after pan of boiling water.
(Or polio, or cancer)
    Kids warned not to run about.
(It wasn't murder on the sand dunes)
    Only half full, but scalding
(It wasn't drowning in the canal)
    When she tripped and fell in.

That's me on the left.
Lucky horseshoe still trailing.
That's Dorothy, still seven.

Casablanca

You must remember this
To fall in love in Casablanca
To be the champion of Morocco.

The size of tuppence
Photographs show Uncle Bill holding silver cups
Wearing sepia silks and a George Formby grin.

Dominique
Had silent film star looks. With brown eyes
Black hair and lips full to the brim, she was a race apart.

He brought her over
To meet the family early on. An exotic bloom
In bleak post-war Bootle. Just the once.

Had there been children
There might have been more contact. But letters,
Like silver cups, were few and far between.

At seventy-eight
It's still the same old story. Widowed and lonely
The prodigal sold up and came back home.

I met him that first Christmas
He spoke in broken scouse. Apart from that
He looked like any other bow-legged pensioner.

He had forgotten the jockey part
The fight for love and glory had been a brief episode
In a long, and seemingly, boring life.

It turned out
He had never felt at home there
Not a week went by without him thinking of Liverpool.

Casablanca
The airplane on the runway. She in his arms.
Fog rolling in from the Mersey. As time goes by.

The Wrong Beds

Life is a hospital ward, and the beds we are put in
are the ones we don't want to be in.
We'd get better sooner if put over by the window.
Or by the radiator, one could suffer easier there.

At night, the impatient soul dreams of faraway places.
The Aegean: all marble and light. Where, upon a beach
as flat as a map, you could bask in the sun like a lizard.

The Pole: where, bathing in darkness, you could watch
the sparks from Hell reflected in a sky of ice. The soul
could be happier anywhere than where it happens to be.

Anywhere but here. We take our medicine daily,
nod politely, and grumble occasionally.
But it is out of our hands. Always the wrong place.
We didn't make our beds, but we lie in them.

My Shadow is but a Shadow of Its Former Self

It was in Kalgoorlie last year, late one afternoon
the sun scorching my back, when, there at my feet
not a silhouette of anthracite, not a steam-rollered
Giacometti, but a gauze veil. A finely pencilled sketch.

I blamed the tinnies and thought no more about it.
But this summer, while jogging in Battersea Park,
I noticed that whenever I sprinted, my shadow fell behind
and I had to stop and wait for it to catch up.

I have also noticed that when the sunblock wears off
so does my shadow. Am I becoming translucent?
At midnight I play statues on the lawn. The moon
sees through me, but gives the cat a familiar to play with.

I fear that summertime when I will keep to the house
and feel my way around darkened rooms.
Dozing in armchairs, I will avoid the bedroom, where,
propped up on pillows and fading, waits my shadow.

Perfume

I lack amongst other things a keen sense of smell.
Coffee I have no problem with. It leads me
by the nose into the kitchen each morning
before vanishing at first sip.

And cheap scent? Ah, bonsoir!
How many lamp-posts have I
almost walked into, senses blindfolded,
lost in the misdemeanours of time?

At twenty paces I can sniff the difference
between a vindaloo and a coq au vin.
Weak at the knees, I will answer
the siren call of onions sizzling,

Sent reeling, punch-drunk on garlic.
No, it's the subtleties that I miss.
Flowers. Those free gifts laid out
on Mother Nature's perfume counter.

Sad but true, roses smell red to me
(even white ones). Violets blue.
Everything in the garden, though lovely,
might as well be cling-filmed.

If I close my eyes and you hold up
a bloom, freshly picked, moist with dew,
I smell nothing. Your fingers perhaps?
Oil of Ulay? Nail varnish?

Then describe in loving detail its pinkness,
the glowing intensity of its petals,
and I will feel its warm breath upon me,
the distinctive scent of its colour.

Those flowers you left in the bedroom
a tangle of rainbows spilling from the vase.
Gorgeous. I turn off the light.
Take a deep breath. Smell only darkness.

Half-term

Half-term holiday, family away
Half-wanting to go, half-wanting to stay
Stay in bed for half the day.

Half-read, half-listen to the radio
Half-think things through. Get up,
Half-dressed, half-wonder what to do.

Eat half a loaf, drink half a bottle
(Save the other half until later).
Other half rings up. Feel better.

Light Sleeper

My wife is such a light sleeper
That when I come home late
After a night out with the boys
I always remove my shoes
And leave them at the bottom
Of the street.

Imagine my surprise, when
On retrieving them this morning
I discovered that they had been
Polished.

What a nice neighbourhood I live in.
What a great country this is.

Posh

Where I live is posh
  Sundays the lawns are mown
My neighbours drink papaya squash

Sushi is a favourite nosh
  Each six-year-old has a mobile phone
Where I live is posh

In spring each garden is awash
  with wisteria, pink and fully blown
My neighbours drink papaya squash

Radicchio thrives beneath the cloche
  Cannabis is home grown
Where I live is posh

Appliances by Míele and Bosch
  Sugar-free jam on wholemeal scone
My neighbours drink papaya squash

Birds hum and bees drone
  The paedophile is left alone
My neighbours drink papaya squash
Where I live is posh.

Coach and Horses

One of those poems you write in a pub
on a wet Friday. On your own and nothing to read.
Surrounded by people hugging each other with language.

But you are not without a friend in the world.
You are not here simply for the Alc. 5.5% Vol.
To prove it, you appear to have had a sudden thought.

Writing, like skinning beermats, is displacement activity.
You word-doodle with crazed concentration,
feigning oblivion to the conversations that mill around.

The seductive, the leery, arm in arm with the slurred
and the weary. For some reason, possibly alcoholic,
the doodles coalesce into a train of thought.

Actively displaced, you race along the platform
as it gathers speed. But before you can jump aboard
Time is called, and it comes off the rails.

But this is your secret. Unacknowledged legislator,
you drink up and leave, with a poem so full of holes
you could drive a coach and horses through it.

Nothing ventured
I rise from my hangover
And take a walk along the towpath.

The wind is acting plain silly
And the sky, having nobody to answer to
Is all over the place.

The Thames (as it likes to be called)
Gives a passable impersonation of a river
But I remain unimpressed.

Suddenly in front of me, a woman.
We are walking at the same pace.
Lest she thinks I'm following her, I quicken mine.

She quickens hers. I break into a run.
So does she. It's looking bad now.
I'm gaining on her. God, what happens

When I catch up? Luckily, she trips
And sprawls headlong into a bed of nettles.
I sprint past with a cheery 'Hello'.

Out of sight, I leave the path and scramble
Down to the water's edge, where I lie down
And pretend to be a body washed ashore.

There is something very comforting
About being a corpse. My cares float away
Like non-biodegradable bottles.

A cox crows. The crew slams on its oars
And a rowing boat rises out of the water
To teeter on splintering legs like a drunken tsetse fly.

Before it can be disentangled
And put into reverse, a miracle: Lazarus risen,
Is up and away along the towpath.

Near Hammersmith Bridge, the trainer
Is on the other foot, as a hooded figure,
Face in shadow, comes pounding towards me.

A jogger? A mugger?
A mugger whose hobby is jogging? Vice-versa?
(Why do such men always have two *g*'s?)

I search in vain for a bed of nettles.
No need. She sprints past with a cheery 'Hello'.
I recognize the aromatherapist from Number 34.

★　★　★

Waiting beneath the bridge for my breath
To catch up, I hear a cry. A figure is leaning
Out over the river, one hand on the rail.

His screaming is sucked into the slipstream
Of roaring traffic. On the walkway, pedestrians
Hurry past like Bad Samaritans.

I break into a sweat and run,
Simultaneously. 'Hold on,' I cry, 'hold on.'
Galvanized, I'm up the stairs and at his side.

The would-be suicide is a man in his late twenties,
His thin frame shuddering with despair,
His eyes, clenched tattoos: HATE, HATE.

My opening gambit is the tried and trusted:
'Don't jump!' He walks straight into the cliché-trap.
'Leave me alone, I want to end it all.'

I ask him why? 'My wife has left me.'
My tone is sympathetic. 'That's sad,
But it's not the end of the world.'

'And I'm out of work and homeless.'
'It could be worse,' I say, and taking his arm
Firmly but reassuringly, move in close.

'If you think you're hard done by
You should hear what I've been through.
Suffering? I'll tell you about suffering.'

We are joined by a man in a blue uniform.
'I can handle this,' I snarl.
'You get back to your parking tickets.'

He turns out to be a major
In the Salvation Army, so I relent
And let him share the intimacy of the moment.

I explain the loneliness that is for ever
The fate of the true artist,
The icy coldness that grips the heart.

The black holes of infinite despair
Through which the sensitive spirit must pass.
The seasons in Hell. The flowers of Evil.

The tide was turning and a full moon rising
As I lighted upon the existentialist nightmare,
The chaos within that gives birth to the dancing star.

I was illustrating the perpetual angst and ennui
With a recent poem, when the would-be suicide
jumped –
                (First)

The Sally Army officer, four stanzas later.
I had done my best. I dried my tears,
Crossed the road and headed west.

On the way home, needless to say, it rained.
My hangover welcomed me with open arms.
Nothing gained.

In Good Spirits

This icy winter's morning
I rise in good spirits.

On all fours I exhale
a long white breath
that hangs in the air
like a shimmering rope.

Under which, with arms akimbo
and eyes ablaze, I dance the limbo.

The Perfect Place

The world is the perfect place to be born into.
Unless of course, you don't like people
or trees, or stars, or baguettes.

Its secret is movement.
As soon as you have stepped back
to admire the scenery
or opened your mouth
to sing its praises
it has changed places with itself.

Infinitesimally, perhaps,
but those infinitesimals add up.

(About the baguettes,
that was just me being silly.)

Clutching at Cheese Straws

Out of my depth at the cocktail party
I clutch at cheese straws.
'Why are they called straws, do you think?'

Treading water, the ice-cool blonde
raises an eyebrow and shrugs.
'I mean, you can't drink through them.'

A second eyebrow reaches for the sky.
'Or is it because they taste like straw?'
A pause, and then she says:

'I assume it's the shape, don't you?'
Holding my breath, I take the plunge
and resurface with a crown of twiglets.

'Why are these called . . . ?' But she has been rescued.
Weighed down, I wade down to the shallow end
and help the lads keep aloft

A giant, inflatable hammer.

In Vain

I like liposuction, I've had my lipo sucked.
No flab to grab on my abdomen
My buttocks neatly tucked.

Implants in my pectorals, wrinkles all erased
Nosejob and a hairpiece, both eyes doubleglazed.
Zits all zapped by laser, cheekbones smashed and reset.
But sadly, my days are numbered,
I'm up to my ears . . .
Remember how they used to stick out? . . . in debt.

(For in brackets here I'll mention
A certain *glandular* extension)
Penile, in fact, which increased my libido
Though senile I act like a beast
And the need, oh the greed,
Oh those nights of seedless passion!

Which will doubtless explain
The cardiovascular pain
And three-way bypass, alas, in vain.

Wearing pyjamas designed by Armani
A perfect body waiting to die.
Bewigged, butchered and bewildered
Am I,
     Am I,
          Am I.

Clone

A genetic scientist
With literary leanings
Cloned old verses
And gave them new meanings

A genetic scientist
With literary leanings
Cloned old verses
And gave them new meanings

A genetic scientist
With literary leanings
Cloned old verses
And gave them new meanings

The Health Forecast

Well, it's been a disappointing day
in most parts, has it not?
So, let's have a look at tomorrow's charts
and see what we've got.

Let's start with the head, where tonight
a depression centred over the brain
will lift. Dark clouds move away
and pain will be widespread but light.

Exposed areas around the neck and shoulders
will be cold (if not wearing a vest)
and there may be dandruff on high ground
especially in the west.

Further inland:
Tomorrow will begin with a terrible thirst.
Lungs will be cloudy at first,
in some places for most of the day,
and that fog in the throat
simply won't go away.
So keep well wrapped up, won't you?

For central areas the outlook is fairly bright
although the liver seems unsettled
after a heavy night,
and a belt of high pressure, if worn too tight,
may cause discomfort.

Further south it will be mainly dry
although showers are expected in private parts
and winds will be high,
reaching gale force incontinent.
Some thunder.

Around midnight, this heavy front
is expected to move in,
resulting in cyclonic highs
in and around the upper thighs.
Temperatures will rise
and knees may well seize up in the heat.
And as for the feet,
perspiration will be widespread
resulting in a sweaty bedspread.

And the outlook for the weak?
Not as good as for the strong, I'm afraid.
Goodnight.

New brooms sweep clean
Old brooms can't be fussed
New brooms are mad keen
Old brooms can't stand dust.

New brooms are young bulls
Can't wait to get their teeth
Into the kitchen carpet,
Up the stairs and underneath

The fridge and the cooker
Where grease stains won't dissolve,
With each problem their bristles
Stiffening with resolve.

Old brooms are allergic
To dust and doggy hair
Than raise a whirlwind in the lounge
They would much prefer

To rearrange the particles
With a reassuring sweep,
Then lean against the cupboard wall
For a long and dreamless sleep.

'Dust is the carpet of the contented'
The motto of ancient brooms
And of the folk who sit contentedly
Waiting, in darkening rooms.

Dressed for the Occasion

I have enough jackets and trousers
Though shirts I may need to replace
A couple of suits I can oxfam
As they take up far too much space.

One overcoat, one jacket, leather,
One linen suit for summer weather
Hats of course, and a dressing-gown
Should last until the blind comes down.

One Poet May Hide Another

(for Kenneth Koch)

Kenya
A car held up at a railroad crossing
At the wheel, the poet.
To pass the time he writes a poem.

London
Holed up in his study, a second poet
Reads the poem, then ducks.
He realizes that it may hide another.

However
He is unprepared for the train
That comes hurtling out of the fireplace
Followed by another, and another, and

On the train to Bangor from Crewe
Jo Shapcott and I, as tutors tend to do
gossip, and get to wonder

which of the passengers are headed
for Ty Newydd. That orange-haired
punk in tight leather? Unlikely.

More likely the old lady wearing purple
(see Jenny Joseph), daring people
to come close, if any do, they're kissed.

Or, pissed in the corner, surrounded
by throttled cans of Guinness,
the man who shakes a mottled fist

at a muse unseen, and screams:
'Orange, orange, there must be
a rhyme for feckin' orange!'

For the Sake of Argument

The cover of this book is yellow
But, for the sake of argument
Let us call it red.

It goes without saying that you are alive
But, for the sake of argument
Let us say you are dead.

And not only dead but buried
The headstone smeared with dirt.
(Don't take offence, it's merely polemic

You pretentious little squirt.
You self-regarding upstart
You couldn't write if you tried).

So, for the sake of argument
Let's settle this outside.

★　　★　　★

Between the writer and the reader
Somewhere the meaning floats
And, waiting on the sidelines,
The poem holds the coats.

The Written Word

(a Full Monty of poetic forms)

A poet of little repute
  Desperate for something to do
One evening pissed as a newt
  Decided to have a tattoo.

On his chest an unrhymed sestina
  On his belly a fine villanelle
On each bicep a series of haiku
  On each shank a tanka as well.

On each shoulder a Petrarchan sonnet
  Making twenty-eight lines in all
An acrostic across each firm buttock
  With a limerick, what else? on each ball.

On each knee, though knobbly, a rondeau redoublé
  (which was terribly tricky to do)
On each pendulous lobe, a Pindaric ode
  On each clavicle, a neat clerihew.

Any flesh that remained was minutely quatrained
  (the odd couplet if not enough room)
On the sole of each foot, a virelai was put
  An englyn and Malaysian pantoum.

* * *

This poet of Great Repute
   Now travels from town to town
Goes on stage, removes his shirt
   And takes his trousers down.

While audiences marvel
   At the body of work so vast
Concrete, surreal and post-modern
   Alongside the great works of the past.

And some are poetry-lovers
   Who believe they could do worse
Than curl up every evening
   With this anthology of verse.

For nothing can beat the written word
Especially on a torso, bared.

Trust Me, I'm a Poet

Your husband upped and left you
After years of playing the field?
My heart goes out, I know the type
Of course, my lips are sealed.
Let me be your confidant
I'm generous, let me show it
Champagne, I think is called for
Trust me, I'm a poet.

★　　★　　★

Put my wallet on the counter
When I turned round it had gone
And I've got to meet my agent
In town, for lunch at one
To sign a five-book contract
I'll be back before you know it
Can you lend me fifty quid?
Trust me, I'm a poet.

A Literary Riddle

I am

Out of my tree

Away with the fairies

A nut. A fruitcake. What am I?

Answer: One line short of a cinquain.

Tonight will be an ordinary poetry reading
A run-of-the-mill kind of affair
Nothing that will offend or challenge
No *language* as far as I'm aware.

The poets are thoroughly decent
All vetted by our committee
We had hoped Wendy Cope might appear
But she's tied up more's the pity.

And that other one, whose name I forget . . .
Quite famous . . . Recently died . . .
He'd have been good. But never mind,
At least we can say that we tried.

Personally, I prefer actors
Reading the Great Works of the Past
The trouble with poets is they mumble
Get nervous, and then speaktoofast.

And alcohol is a danger
So that's been kept well out of sight
As long as they're sober this evening
They can drink themselves legless all night.

By the way, they've come armed with slim volumes
Which of course, they're desperate to sell
Otherwise, there's coffee in the foyer
With KitKats and Hobnobs as well.

Well, I think that covers everything
All that remains for me to say
Is to wish you . . . an ordinary evening
Such a pity I'm unable to stay.

Dialectically Opposed

In Bristol, to escape the drizzle
One November afternoon, I ventured
Into a large book shop, George's,
Opposite the university where I was
To read that same evening.

It was my custom in those days
To sniff out my slim volumes
And give them due prominence.
Covers outfacing, three or four titles
Would see off most of the opposition.

But on this occasion, try as I might
(and I might have tried harder),
I could find no poetry whatsoever.
Then I spotted the Information Desk
Behind which was a girl with large bristols.

(I mention this, not to be sexist
But to remind you of that fair city.)
'Excuse me,' I said. 'Do you have
a Poetry Section?' Rose-Marie replied:
'I think you'll find it under Livestock.'

I stood, quandried to the spot.
'Livestock? Poetry? Books of Verse?'
The penny dropped. I watched its descent
Into the perfumed gorge of Avon.
'Poeltry,' she laughed. 'I thought you said Poultry!'

A Serious Poem

This is a serious poem
It wears a serious face
It will not fritter away the words
It knows its place.

Perfectly balanced
Neither too long nor too short
It gazes solemnly heavenwards
Like a real poem ought.

Familiar with the classics
It drops names with ease.
Here comes Plato with Lycidas
And look, there's Demosthenes!

A serious poem will often end
With two lines that rhyme.
But not always.

Ee Bah Gum

Spare a thought for your grandmother
who would sit me on her knee
(she had just the one), and tell ee
bah gum stories of days gone by.

'Ee bah gum, it were reet tough,'
she would say, 'workin at mill
from dawn until dusk,
and all for a measly ten shillin a week.'

The thought of clogs and cobbled streets
of matchstick men and smoking chimneys
would bring a tear to her eye,
(she had just the one), then, brightening:

'Mind you, in those days you could buy a nice house,
end-of-terrace for sixpence,
and for a fortnight in Blackpool
you got change out of a farthing.'

Spare a thought for your grandmother
who married well and wanted lots
and lots of children (she had just the one),
and so bequeathed to me, her Lowrys.

The Wreck of the *Hesperus*

'You look like the wreck of the *Hesperus*
How long is it since you slept?'
As through the whistling sleet and snow
Like a sheeted ghost she swept.

'Where have you been until this hour
In roughest gale and stinging blast?'
Then wrapping her warm in his seaman's coat
He lay her down to rest.

'The least you could have done was ring
you knew I'd be worried sick.'
With rattling shrouds all sheathed in ice
She drifted, a dreary wreck.

'You promised on your mother's grave.
Why, oh why?' he cried.
But like the horns of an angry bull
The cruel rocks gored her side.

'Let me comb the seaweed from your hair
Come hither, daughter mine.'
But her brain was soft as carded wool
And her heart was caked with brine.

'Sleep tight,' said he. 'Sweet dreams,' said he,
'For soon the sun will rise.'
But the salt sea was frozen on her breast
The salt tears in her eyes.

Washed up was she, at break of day
(Christ save us all from a death like this)
On the bleak beach of the carpet lay
For she was the wreck of the *Hesperus*.
For she was the wreck of the *Hesperus*.

The Revenge of My Last Duchess

Downstairs, Neptune taming the sea-horses, let us descend.
The Count your master is generous and I seek his daughter's hand.

My first wife was put to death, at my command some say
I thought to reason with her, but that is not our way.

My name, after all, is nine hundred years old
She never appreciated that, and worse, her looks were bold.

Her eyes went everywhere and her smiles were cheap
Other men she whispered to, while moving in her sleep.

Bringing their lives, unwittingly, to an agonizing end.
Yes, even the painter of the portrait before which we stand.

Why do you ask? You pale. Why do you look alarmed?
A dagger raised? For pity's sake I am unarmed.

You cry vengeance. I beg, sir, what harm have I done?
Frà Pandolf! Oh God, I see him now, you are his son!

Stop All the Cars

(The Metro, 1980–1998, RIP)

Stop all the cars, cut off the ignition
Those who decide have made the decision
Muffle the exhaust, put flowers in the boot
Wear a black dress or a morning suit.

Let the traffic lights remain on red
Jam the horns out of respect for the dead
Sound the Last Post and summon the guard
For the Metro has gone to the knacker's yard.

She was my rustbucket, my tin lizzie
She kept my garage mechanic busy
A tarnished icon of the Thatcher years
She ground to a halt as I ground the gears.

Traffic wardens openly break down and weep
Sleeping policemen stir in their sleep
Car thieves consider an easier trade
Ram-raiders can't be bothered to raid.

Close the motorways with black-ribboned cones
Riddle the ashes and rattle the bones
Sound the Last Post and summon the guard
For the Metro has gone to the knacker's yard.

I don't believe that one about the butterfly –
The air displaced by the fluttering
of its wings in Brazil
causing a tidal wave in Bangladesh.

Mind you,
The day after I shook out
a tablecloth on the patio
there was an earthquake in Mexico.

(Or was it the other way round?)

Global Warming

In the Antarctic, an ice-shelf
Twice the size of Norfolk
Has broken off, and is melting.

People the world over are concerned
Especially those in Suffolk
Who always get the thin end of the wedge.

Sheer

Cliff faces do not like the word 'sheer'
Especially those who are afraid of heights.
One day, you are a rising upland,
a grassy ridge overlooking vales and hills
that roll gently toward the distant sea

And the next, the distant sea has crept up
behind you. A crack, an ice-pick
into the skull of your nearest and dearest
and there you are, thrust to the fore,
up to your knees in stinging foam.

Don't look down. Keep your eyes fixed
on the horizon. Ignore the squealing,
dizzy flight of gulls. The squalls,
the gales that smack, the nails that scratch.
An era or two and you'll get used to it.

Even come to enjoy your position. Looked up to
and admired, surveyed and photographed.
Until, when you least expect it, the earth sighs,
a fractal blip, and you sheer away into the sea.
Today, a proud headland, tomorrow, oceanography.

The Sad Astronomer

The astronomer is sad.
Unconsolable. Last night
a freak tornado
tore through the village,
destroying the observatory.

His telescope is beyond repair.
Tonight he opens the sky
but cannot read it.
The stars, a jumble,
dance before his eyes.

The Mandarin Hotel, Jakarta.
5-star, bordering on the Milky Way.
Bathrobes a polar bear would kill for,
slippers I slide about in still.
A bowl with fruit so exotic,
you need a licence to peel,
and instructions on how to eat.
A bed as big as this room.

Attached to a cellophaned bouquet of flowers,
that looks too dangerous to unwrap,
a card from the Hotel Manager
who welcomes me (misspelling my name).
He telephones: Could we be photographed
together for the Hotel Magazine?
Puzzled, flattered and vaguely disquieted,
I agree. Within minutes
I am holding a glass of champagne,
his arm around my shoulder,
flicking through my limited series of smiles.

Then the inevitable: I am not
who he thought I was. I am not
who I am supposed to be.
He laughs it off, apologizes, and leaves,
taking the rest of the champagne with him.

I walk out on to the balcony.
From the 37th floor the city seeps
towards the horizon like something spilled.
Something not nice. That might stain.

I go back inside. Examine my passport,
and get out the photographs.
A couple who could be anybody
against a wall that could be anywhere.
A dog. Children smiling.

I unwrap the flowers. Open the maxi-bar.

Balloon Fight

'This morning, the American, Steve Fossett, ended his Round-the-World balloon fight . . . I'm sorry, balloon "flight" . . . in northern India.'
                    – *The Today Programme*, Radio 4, 20 January 1997

It ended in Uttar Pradesh.
It had to.
You can't go around the world
attacking people with balloons
and expect to get away with it.

What may be mildly amusing
at children's parties
in Upper Manhattan
will not seem so funny ha ha
on the Falls Road.

How Fossett fought his way
across the former Yugoslavia
I'll never know.
Some folk never grow up.
Hang on to their childhood.

Believing in the Tooth Fairy,
watched over by the Man in the Moon.
Thank you, Mr Newsreader,
for bringing him down to earth.
For bursting his balloon.

The Map

Wandering lost and lonely in Bologna
I found a street-map on the piazza.
Unfortunately, it was of Verona.

As I was refolding it into a limp concertina,
A voice: 'Ah, you've found it! I'm Fiona,
Let me buy you a spritzer, over there on the terrazza.'

Two spritzers later we ordered some pasta
(Bolognese, of course, then zabaglione).
I felt no remorse, merely amore.

Proposing a toast to love at first sight
We laughed and talked over a carafe of chianti
When out of the night, like a ghost, walked my aunty.

'Look who's here,' she cried. 'If it isn't our Tony,
Fancy bumping into you in Italy,
With a lady friend too,' then added, bitterly:

'How are Lynda and the kids? I'm sure they're OK.
While the mice are at home the tomcat will play.'
A nod to Fiona, 'Nice to meet you. Ciao!'

I snapped my grissini. 'Stupid old cow!'
Then turned to Fiona. She was no longer there.
Our romance in tatters, like the map on her chair.

Whoops!

You are strangely excited
as we enter the crowded bar
and find a small table in the corner.

You insist on fetching the drinks
and before disappearing
squeeze a note into my hand.

It reads: 'Why go home tonight?
I have a room. I have a bed.
I have a spare toothbrush.'

I recognize my own handwriting.

Fits and Starts

His love life is one of fits and starts
   Claims he works as 'something in the City'
(partly true, he works at Marks & Sparks)

Engaged once to a student nurse at Bart's
   Who broke it off ('He's sad, a sort of Walter Mitty')
His love life is one of fits and starts

Twice a week he goes with dodgy tarts
   Half his wages on the nitty-gritty
(though not, it must be said, at Marks & Sparks)

Life can be the pits, and it's a pity
   To distil one little life into a ditty.
On your marks: his love life is one of
   Fits and starts – If it fits, it starts.

In Case of Fire

In case of FIRE break glass
In case of GLASS fill with water
In case of WATER wear heavy boots
In case of HEAVY BOOTS assume foetal position
In case of FOETAL POSITION loosen clothing
In case of CLOTHING avoid nudist beach
In case of NUDIST BEACH keep sand out of eyes
In case of EYES close curtains
In case of CURTAINS switch on light
In case of LIGHT embrace truth
In case of TRUTH spread word
In case of WORD keep mum
In case of MUM open arms
In case of ARMS lay down gun
In case of GUN, fire
In case of FIRE break glass.

Vague Assumptions

I assume that the fire started before
    the fire-brigade arrived
I assume that the neighbours did not put on pyjamas
    and nightdresses to go out into the street
I assume that the woman is not in hysterics
    because the policeman has his arms around her
I assume that the suicide note left by the arsonist
    will not be found among the ashes

I assume that the siren's wail has nothing to do
    with the unhappiness of the ambulance
I assume that continentals drive on the right
    because foreign cars have the steering-wheel on the left
I assume that wing mirrors are a godsend
    to angels who care about good grooming
I assume that to a piece of flying glass
    one eye is as good as another

I assume that if the sun wasn't there for the earth to revolve around
    there would be fewer package holidays
I assume that a suitcase becomes heavy
    only when lifted
I assume that water boils
    only when the bubbles tell it to
I assume that because the old lady died
    the operation to save her life as a baby had not been successful

I assume that the bundle of rags asleep in Harrods' doorway
    is not queuing for the January sales
I assume that the people waiting in line for the DSS to open,
    do not work there
I assume that the people lying on the floor of the bank
    are not taking it easy
I assume that the hooded figure wielding a gun at the counter
    is not opening an account

I assume that to claim the reward
    one must hand over the kitten
I assume that the shopping-trolley on the beach
    has not been washed ashore from a deep-sea supermarket
I assume that to achieve wisdom
    one must arrive after the event
I assume that by the time you read this
    I will have written it.

Shite

Where I live is shite
  An inner-city high-rise shack
Social workers shoot on sight

The hospital's been set alight
  The fire brigade's under attack
Where I live is shite

Police hide under their beds at night
  Every road's a cul-de-sac
Social workers shoot on sight

Girls get pregnant just for spite
  My mate's a repo-maniac
Where I live is shite

Newborn junkies scratch and bite
  Six-year-olds swap sweets for crack
Social workers shoot on sight

Tattooed upon my granny's back
  A fading wrinkled Union Jack
Social workers shoot on sight
Where I live is shite.

Old-fashioned Values

I have old-fashioned values
Prefer things the way they used to be
When good manners were a premium
And there was a sense of community

Front doors could be left wide-open
And children play out in the street
Everyone on first-name terms
With the bobby on his beat

No beggars huddled in doorways
No muggers in the dark
No syringes in the stairwells
No rapists in the park

On a crowded bus a man would stand
To offer a lady his seat
Vegetables came fresh from the land
There was gravy and innocent meat

No holes in the ozone layer
No AIDS or BSE
No serial killers in Gloucester
No violence on TV

I have old-fashioned values
Prefer things the way they used to be
When the world wore a smile
And I was young, in nineteen eighty-three.

Sometimes I wish I was back in Nicosia
smoking the wacky-backy with the lads
and watching Sandy getting tarted up.

Night on the town. Blood on the streets.
Razor-blades stitched into the lapels
of his crushed-velvet tartan jacket.

Headcase but funny with it. Not like Fitzy.
Now we're talking nasty bastards.
Four brothers and half a brain between them.

He only knew three questions:
Who are you lookin at? What did you say?
Are you takin the piss?

Simple questions that no one ever got right
because only Fitzy knew the answers:
(a) Beerglass   (b) Boot   (c) Head-butt.

Put on more charges than the Light Brigade.
Next thing, he marries a local girl.
Maria Somethingopolis. Big name. Big family.

It won't last long, we said. And it didn't.
Took three of them, though. Stabbed him
in the back of a car, then set fire to it.

Cyprus One, England Nil. Mainly, though,
I remember the good times. Sound mates,
cheap bevvy. Moonlight on the Med. End of story.

Spoil-sports

There's always someone who spoils things, isn't there?
We are all enjoying the story
and someone has to shout out something silly.

We are all there in good time
and someone has to be late
spoiling it for everybody else.

There we are, all dressed up, gone to a lot of trouble
and someone has to show up
looking like I don't know what.

They do it on purpose, we know that.
Just to make themselves feel important.

When not destroying plant-life
they're using sawn-off shotguns.
Blowing up aeroplanes
Not paying their TV licences
Throwing my satchel into the canal
Reporting me to Mr Clark, and I hadn't done anything.

★　　★　　★

My wife and I run a little business.
Exotic plants. Carnivores mainly. Venus flytraps,
that sort of thing. The place is always full
and we take the time to explain how,
once trapped within the plant, the insects
are broken down by enzymes and the proteins
extracted, leaving only the decaying husks.
People find it fascinating, especially children.

But as soon as your back is turned
there is always someone who thinks it's funny
to introduce foreign bodies. Chewing-gum,
sweet-wrappers, lolly-ice sticks, pencils,
even a chicken tikka sandwich once.

They do it on purpose, we know that.
Just to be different, just to spoil it for everybody else.

Pen Pals

As you can imagine, a man in my position
Receives a lot of mail. My poor wife, on the other hand,
None at all. Until recently that is

When the postman dropped her a line.
His motives, I am sure, were altruistic,
And her reply, written that same morning,

Prompted by feelings of courtesy.
His letter by return, however, was ripped open
In a manner that could be regarded as unseemly.

And when my wife took breakfast
Locked in her room, composing a reply
I should have spotted the danger signals.

But, being absorbed in various projects, did not.
In fact, I delighted at seeing her fulfilled,
The loose ends of her days gummed down.

It was BURMA at the beginning of the third week
That set the alarm bells ringing. Although
Not widely travelled, I am a man of the world

And the thought of My Angel, Being Undressed
And Ready for Postman Pat spurred me into action.
Our nearest pillar-box is at the end of the road

And that morning I crouched behind it, until,
Just before noon, she approached, the ink not yet dry.
And as she offered the profane wafer to its iron lips

I leaped out and snatched it from her grasp.
In the privacy of my rooms I tore open the letter
And confronted her with its contents.

'Pen pals,' she insisted. 'We are only pen pals.'
'Pen pals,' I pointed out, 'don't make plans
To cavort in the back of Delivery Vans.'

I insisted that the relationship be terminated
Immediately, and dictated the following:
'Dear Ken,' (for Ken it was)

'I wish to break off this ludicrous affair,
This adultery-by-proxy. I will have my revenge
You bastard. Yours, Audrey' (for Audrey it was)

'P.S. Another letter to follow.'
I made her post it that same afternoon
And next morning I posted the letterbomb.

The sorting office was out of action for several days
And my wife arrested the following Monday.
But now, thankfully, everything is back to normal.

St Francis and the Lion

The man was sick. He had a history
of mental illness. What he was doing
let loose on the streets we'll never know.
Care in the community they call it.
Wild animals, of course, couldn't care less.

During the summer months the zoo closes
at 8 p.m. It is possible that he got in
after that by scaling the perimeter fence,
but more likely he was already inside,
hiding away, when the keepers locked up.

The lion compound is encircled by a low wall,
a ditch, and a fence seven metres high,
enough to deter even the most athletic
trespasser. The man, however, appears
to have had no trouble in scaling it.

Whether this was a dramatic suicide attempt
or whether he believed he had an empathy
with the beasts is anybody's guess.
Although conclusions may be drawn from the fact
that he was wearing sandals and carrying a Bible.

The victim, who was in his early twenties,
has yet to be identified. Cause of death
would appear to be a broken neck.
The injury consistent with receiving
a single blow from a fully grown male lion.

St Francis and the Lion (II)

We haven't spoken to him since that evening.
As far as we're concerned he's burned his boats.
At first he was all bravado
Trying to justify himself. But it didn't wash.

He knew right away that he'd let us down.
From now on he's on his own
and serves him right. Everybody is upset,
especially the young ones. Let him stew.

We knew that it was St Francis
as soon as he opened his mouth.
He spoke in our language, and beautifully.
Words that were music, that could dance.

But Mali was jealous right from the start.
Yawning, scratching and wandering off,
pretending not to listen. But he did.
You couldn't help but be impressed.

He talked about love and about God
and about how one day, all the fences
would come down and we'd be free
to run wild for ever and ever.

It was then that the devil got into him.
We don't know if it was fear or anger
but whatever it was, he suddenly
let out a roar and sprung upon the boy.

It was over before any of us could move.
No screams. No cries for help.
Motionless he lay. The sun loosening
its grip on the iron bars of the cage.

I suppose, in time, Mali will be forgiven
and he'll return to the pride when the memory
has faded. Already the cynics are whispering . . .
'Mass hysteria . . . Hallucination . . . Once upon a time . . .'

The Father, the Son

It is unusual to find me here, in town.
I never did like crowds. The smell,
The dust, the racket. I can do without it.
But it's a special occasion, and well,
I haven't seen him in a long, long time.

Followed his career with interest, mind.
Well, hardly career, but he's made his mark
They all have, and good on them I say.
The whole country needs shaking up
And they're the boys to do it.

Things are coming to a head now.
History in the making, you can sense it.
That's why I'm here. I may be old
But not too old to lend a hand
Lift a sword and strike a blow for freedom.

Question is, when push comes to shove
Will they stand and fight, or run for it?
They'll not fight alone, that's for sure.
The rank and file will rally round
Even though the odds are stacked against.

Too many leeches with too much to lose
The mobsters, the spies, the black marketeers.
Too many fingers in too many pies.
The backhanders, the sweeteners, the graft
The wheeler-dealers, the sultans of sleaze.

The ones who feed on the carrion of conflict
Who profit from the status quo
Who fuel the hatreds that keep
The tribes apart. Who know
That where there's fear, there's money.

Unless this Jesus can provide the glue
By all accounts he knows a thing or two.
Peace is what he preaches. A coded message
That's clear to understand: There'll be no peace
Until Rome has been driven from this land.

And my son knows that. That's why
He got involved. To fight for the cause.
A chip off the old block and no mistake.
But smarter. Not like his old man, hot-headed.
He likes to plan. Take stock. Cool in a crisis.

Ah, there's something happening now.
Can you hear the cheering? It must be them.
The crowd is ecstatic, and the soldiers,
Under orders, keeping out of the way.
Nervous too, a good sign that, I'd say.

But where's my lad? Ah, there he is
At the back, following at a slower pace.
Looks strangely downcast, I must confess.
But no doubt the sight of his old dad
Will bring a smile to his face . . .
'Judas! . . . Judas!'

On the eleventh morning
Japheth burst into the cabin:
'Dreadful news, everybody, the tigers
have eaten the bambanolas!'

'Oh, not the bambanolas,' cried Mrs Noah.
'But they were my favourites,
all cuddly and furry,
and such beautiful brown eyes.'

Noah took her hand in his.
'Momma, not only were they cute
but they could sing and dance
and speak seven languages.'

'And when baked, their dung was delicious,'
added Shem wistfully.
Everybody agreed that the earth
would be a poorer place without the bambanolas.

Noah determined to look on the bright side.
'At least we still have the quinquasaurapods.'
'Oh, yes, the darling creatures,' said his wife.
'How would we manage without them?'

On deck, one quinquasaurapod was steering,
cooking, fishing, doing a crossword
and finding a cure for cancer.
The other was being stalked by a tiger.

Bad Day at the Ark (II)

One evening while the family were at vespers
From the deck came the sound of furtive whispers.

Impatiently, Ham waited for 'Amen'
Then crept up to investigate with Shem.

Like phantoms in the moonlight, glistening with slime
Two giant slugs were ranting, horns swaying in time:

Sluggy deluge sluggy dark, Sluggy voyage sluggy ark
Sluggy seasick sluggy sneeze, Sluggy splinters sluggy fleas
Sluggy Noah sluggy wife, Sluggy boring sluggy life

Each feculent slug was as huge as a rhino
And smelled of old corpses rolled up in lino.

Clammy, putrescent, oozing mucus and goo
The Creator's revenge locked one night in the loo.

Sluggy bellow sluggy bleat, Sluggy twitter sluggy tweet
Sluggy roar sluggy meow, Sluggy bow sluggy wow
Sluggy quack sluggy moo, Sluggy sink the sluggy crew

'Not only ugly, out of tune and glutinous
These beasts are revolting,' said Shem, 'and mutinous.

Let's do the deed and do it big time
You get the sea–salt, I'll get the quick–lime.'

Sluggy quick-lime, sluggy salt, Sluggy human's sluggy fault
Sluggy melting, sluggy pain, Endangered species down the drain
No one loves a sluggy slug, Gluggy gluggy glug glug glug

Noah, on hearing of the creatures' cruel demise,
Summoned his sons and frowning said, 'Now guys

Our job is to save life, so you're way off the mark
To make a floating abattoir out of an ark.

This cannot go unpunished, and so tonight,
No custard with your apple pie, all right?

Let that be a lesson,' adding with a smirk,
'Giant slugs? Good riddance. Now get back to work.'

Bad Day at the Ark (III)

'They've struck again,' said Mrs Noah, disconsolate.
'A Duck-billed Reindeer this time.
A doe. She had no chance, poor mite.
Sucked dry and covered in pollen,
she lay on deck like a squeezed shammy leather,
little Bambi, whimpering at her side.'

'Those Killer Butterflies will have to go,'
said Noah. 'With a wing-span of twelve metres
and heads the size of mammoths,
they are a liability to everyone on board.
Compared to these Cabbage White vampires
the Giant Bees were pussycats.'

'And functional,' pointed out his wife,
squeezing her toes into the luxurious pile
of the black and yellow striped carpet.
'Mind you, those diaphanous wings
would make a smashing pair of window-blinds
for the nursery. Shall I give the lads a call?'

She picked up the skull of a ring-tailed
maraca and shook it vigorously.
Ham, Shem and Japheth came running,
armed to the back teeth and clad
in the bright red armour of the recently boiled
(and now extinct) Giant Lobsters.

'Death to the blood-sucking lepidoptera,'
they cried (in Hebrew), and ran on deck.
But the beasts were nowhere to be seen.
Having mistaken the distant horizon
for a washing-line, they had fluttered off
to perch upon it and perished. (Honest.)

So Mrs Noah did not get the window-blinds
she had set her heart on for the nursery.
But, by way of compensation, her husband
made a fine set of rockers for the cot
using a pair of gleaming ivory tusks
taken from a Giant Sabre-toothed Hamster.

Bad Day at the Ark (IV)

It occurred first to the lemon-haired manatee
(sole survivor of a pair of poolside-dwelling bipeds)
as she and a male barefaced baboon
were in hiding from Shem, who, armed with a carving-knife
fashioned from the horn of a unicorn, was scouring the ship
in search of something tasty and intelligent for supper.

'If this voyage lasts much longer,' she whispered,
'there will be no animals left to do God's bidding
once the flood subsides.' The baboon nodded,
letting his hand fall on to the silken flesh of her thigh.
The manatee removed his hand gently but firmly.
'I think we should call a meeting, don't you?'

The survivors convened that same night in the empty
brontosaurus basket, and what a sorry sight they were:
Gone the fabulous gryphon, the wingèd giraffe.
Gone the prairie dolphin, the golden-voiced terrapin.
'I hate to say this,' confessed the manatee,
'but I really think that God messed up on this one.

To entrust the infamous Noahs with the task
of building an ark and leading us all to safety
was asking for trouble. I mean, just look at them:
purple-scaled, one-eyed, cloven-hoofed non-entities.
They can talk, yes, and they're house-trained
but in terms of evolution they're . . . they're . . .'

She looked to the barefaced baboon for inspiration.
He winked and wiggled his long tongue lasciviously
'. . . they're way down the line.' The animals yelped,
roared and belched in approval. 'We must jump ship
before reaching dry land, otherwise they'll carry on
where they left off, and consume us at the rate of knots.'

As if on cue, the wind dropped suddenly, and the rain
pitter-petered out. 'It has to be tonight,' she warned.
While the baboon and a few of his best primates
barricaded the Noahs into their sleeping-quarters,
the upturned shell of a blue turtle-whale was lowered
upon the now calm waters, boarded and sailed away.

The Ark and all therein perished, but the giant shell
was washed safely ashore, its precious cargo intact.
The animals gave thanks, and then wearily but joyfully
set off to the four corners of the earth to breed and multiply.
And last to leave were the new Adam and Eve –
The lemon-haired manatee and the barefaced baboon.

Acknowledgements

'Posh', 'Poetspotting' and 'The Written Word' were originally published in *Poetry Review*. The author wishes to acknowledge the following sources: 'Stop All the Cars' after W. H. Auden, 'The Wrong Beds' after Charles Baudelaire, 'The Revenge of My Last Duchess' after Robert Browning, 'In Case of Fire' after Jenny Lewis and 'The Wreck of the *Hesperus*' after Henry Wadsworth Longfellow.